# ryan sheckler

## the real life of a Hot Skater

the real life of

kimberly nicholas

# ryan
# sheckler

## a Hot Skater

BERKLEY BOULEVARD BOOKS, NEW YORK

# Introduction

**If you're a** Ryan Sheckler fan, you've probably watched his reality show on MTV, seen his picture in magazines, and Googled his name on the Internet. But do you know how Ryan first started skateboarding? Where he likes to hang out during his "down time"? What he looks for in a girlfriend?

This scrapbook collection of must-have Ryan Sheckler photos brings you up close and personal with the life of a hot skater, and introduces you to the real sweet and supercool guy behind the star.

# Growing Up Ryan

## Ryan was born to skateboard.

*I*t all started on December 30, 1989, when the future skating phenom was born in La Palma, California, to Randy and Gretchen Sheckler. Only eighteen months later, Ryan would discover his dad's Tony Alva skateboard in the garage of their San Clemente home. Randy placed his son on the board and soon the toddler was pushing himself around with his knee. The rest is history.

In the coming years, as the family grew to include Ryan's brothers, Shane and Kane, Ryan's skills took off. When he was just four years old, his grandma bought him his very own Woody Woodpecker skateboard (too cute!) and two years later he decided he wanted to turn pro someday. With six skate parks near his home, he had plenty of places to try out his moves. One of those spots was the famous Encinitas YMCA, where Ryan used to watch superstars Tony Hawk and Bucky Lasek land some gnarly tricks. Ryan has always looked up to Tony, especially. So for his seventh birthday, Ryan's dad asked Tony to make an appearance at Ryan's birthday party. Tony agreed . . . as long as he could have a piece of chocolate cake. Needless to say, Tony got his cake, and Ryan had the best birthday surprise ever!

[ *A year later, Ryan started competing.* ]

Even with all of the time he spent skating, his parents made sure to keep him grounded. The young hotshot still had to do his chores every week and make sure he finished his schoolwork. Ryan still thanks his parents for keeping him levelheaded and for teaching him what matters most. His family always comes first.

That's one of the reasons his parents' divorce hit him so hard. It's been tough for Ryan to deal with the fact that his family will never quite be the same. But Ryan's determined to maintain a strong bond with both of his parents and to keep things as normal as possible for his little brothers. Now that his dad has moved out, Ryan's the man of the house and those responsibilities are his top priority!

Ryan's family always comes first.

# Get to Know Ryan's Family

## Gretchen Sheckler

* Devoted mom

* All business when she's working as Ryan's manager

* Makes sure that Ryan stays grounded

* Would love it if Ryan found someone like his friend Taylor to date

* Does her best to keep the boys strong during her painful divorce

## Randy Sheckler

* Proud father

* Responsible for Ryan's interest in skateboarding

* Runs several businesses

* His training as a mechanical engineer came in handy when building a skate park in the family's backyard

* Works to keep a strong relationship with his sons, now that he's out of the house

# Shane Sheckler

- ✦ Nicknamed "T-Bone"

- ✦ Three years younger than Ryan

- ✦ An accomplished skateboarder, but not interested in following in Ryan's footsteps

- ✦ Enjoys wrestling and hanging out with his friends

- ✦ Likes to keep things mellow—doesn't want the pressure of his brother's competitive lifestyle

# Kane Sheckler

- ✦ Nicknamed "Vol-Kane-O"

- ✦ Eleven years younger than Ryan

- ✦ Enjoys skateboarding and riding his Razor Scooter with his brothers

- ✦ Idolizes Ryan and his rock-star lifestyle

- ✦ Loves bikes and motorcycles

# A Skater's Life

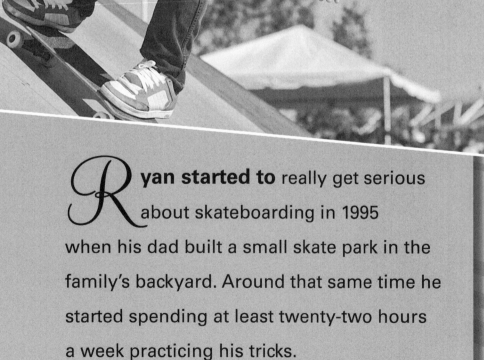

**R**yan **started to** really get serious about skateboarding in 1995 when his dad built a small skate park in the family's backyard. Around that same time he started spending at least twenty-two hours a week practicing his tricks.

*By the age of seven,
Ryan was ready to compete.*

He joined the California Amateur Skateboarding League and started winning their state championships. It wasn't long before he picked up his first sponsor, Arnette, the same eyewear company that had also backed Ryan's hero, Tony Hawk. After winning six amateur titles, it was time for Ryan to turn pro.

At thirteen years old, Ryan became the youngest skateboarder to ever go professional. That year he ripped it up, winning five major events, including the 2003 X Games. He took home the gold in the street competition where he was the only skater to land every trick he attempted. He broke records, becoming the youngest competitor to ever win an X Games gold medal.

Ryan continues to take the skating world by storm. He won the title of National Street Champion in the 2004 and 2005 World Cup of Skateboarding and was named Athlete of the Year by the Dew Action Sports Tour at age fifteen. For the next two years he would hold the title of AST Dew Tour Skateboard Park Champion. Clearly, he's tough to beat in competition. Even Tony Hawk has been known to have said, "He's one of the best all-around skaters of our time."

Ryan's come a long way from just skating around in his driveway. He has as much discipline, determination, and training as any athlete. Competitions can be fierce and dangerous, and Ryan has already sustained several injuries from the sport, including two broken elbows from the same fall! Even after all the broken bones, Ryan always gets back up on the board. He knows it just comes with the territory of being a professional athlete.

But Ryan's skating life doesn't end on the board. In 2002, he and his parents started Ryan Sheckler Inc. The company was formed to handle his endorsements, his website, and all of his publicity efforts. Just this year, he launched Sheckler Merch, a clothing line geared toward skaters and fans. All of this, combined with his reality show on MTV, has made "Ryan Sheckler" a household name.

# Could You Hang with Ryan at the Skate Park?

**All of Ryan's** closest friends know their way around a skateboard. Could you hold your own in a conversation with them? Would you be able to show Ryan that you, too, are interested in his favorite activity? Complete the quiz below and test your knowledge of Ryan Sheckler's greatest passion.

1. **What's an Ollie?**

   a. **A new, kind of clumsy skater**

   b. **A basic move where the skater taps the tail of the skateboard downward to pop up the nose and go into a jump**

   c. **The name of Ryan's agent**

   d. **The position where you stand with your right foot forward on the board**

2. What's the name of Ryan's signature move?

   a. The Shecky

   b. The Ryanator

   c. The Shecklair

   d. The Backwards Kickflip


3. What's Ryan's favorite place to skate?

   a. His backyard skate park

   b. On any ramp

   c. On the street

   d. None of the above


4. Which of the following companies sponsor Ryan?

   a. Panasonic

   b. Red Bull

   c. Etnies

   d. All of the above

**5.** What's an Indy?

    a. An amateur skater

    b. The name of a skate tournament

    c. A skateboard company that sponsors Ryan

    d. A move where the skater grabs the board between his feet with his back hand

**6.** Where was the first modern skateboard created in 1958?

    a. In a California surf shop, dude!

    b. At a Japanese automaker

    c. In a New Jersey teenager's home

    d. None of the above

**7.** Of the following, which is a pro skater?

    a. Tony Hawk

    b. Paul Rodriguez

    c. Tim O'Connor

    d. All of the above

8. When was skateboarding made an Olympic competition?

    a. 1988

    b. 1980

    c. 2008

    (d.) It hasn't been, but maybe in 2012!

9. What's a kicktail?

    a. It's what Ryan does in competitions—he "kicks" some "tail"!

    b. The ends of the skateboard that turn up

    (c.) A basic move that leads off from the top of a ramp

    d. An obstacle at the skate park

10. What skateboarder invented thirty tricks and is known as the father of modern skateboarding?

    a. Ryan Sheckler

    b. Randy Sheckler

    c. Rodney Mullen

    (d.) Tony Hawk

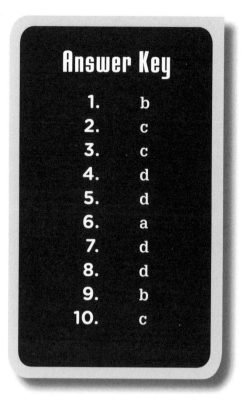

## Answer Key

| | |
|---|---|
| 1. | b |
| 2. | c |
| 3. | c |
| 4. | d |
| 5. | d |
| 6. | a |
| 7. | d |
| 8. | d |
| 9. | b |
| 10. | c |

# How Did You Do?

### If you had 0 to 3 correct answers:

Seriously? You are not ready to hang out with Ryan. Start reading some skating magazines, surf the Internet, and watch more of Ryan's show. Bone up on your skating knowledge and maybe then you won't look completely lost at the skate park.

### If you had 4 to 7 correct answers:

Not terrible, but Ryan's buddies might still suspect that you're a poser. Practice a bit more and Casey and Tony might start inviting you to skate with them.

### If you had 8 to 10 correct answers:

Man, you get mad props for your skating knowledge! You've definitely got what it takes to fit in with Ryan's bros. Ryan may even invite you along to his competitions on the road!

He's one of the best all-around skaters of our time.
—Tony Hawk

# Keeping It Real

**E**ver since his reality series took off, Ryan's been spending a lot of time on the red carpet. *Life of Ryan* was the highest-rated new show on MTV in 2007 with a total of 41 million viewers, so the spotlight on him is shining brighter than ever.

Even outside of his show, Ryan's getting a lot of air time. He's been a guest on *Ellen*, fuse's *The Sauce* and MTV's *TRL*.

On top of all that, he got to show off his family's home on *Cribs*. In between interviews, he's attending photo shoots, appearing at awards shows—like Nickelodeon's Kids' Choice Awards—and even filming a few skating movies. In fact, he has a part in *Street Dreams*, a film written and produced by Rob Dyrdek of MTV's *Rob and Big*, which also stars Ryan's pal Paul Rodriguez.

*There's some definite perks to being a celebrity!*

Ryan's stardom came on fast and strong. Now, he's being followed by paparazzi and making friends with celebrities. His eighteenth birthday party was a star-studded event at the Oakley headquarters that included performances by Lil Jon and Three 6 Mafia. Everywhere he goes, he's rubbing elbows with other big Hollywood names. In fact, there's talk that he's been dating AJ Michalka, one of the sisters in the teen pop duo, Aly and AJ.

Along with the fame comes some serious bling. Ryan admits that he has a weakness for diamonds. He's often seen out on the town with some wicked chains! In addition, he gets tons of cool clothes and gifts from his sponsors. There's some definite perks to being a celebrity!

Still, somehow Ryan manages to remain an ordinary guy living an extraordinary life. Instead of getting caught up in the Hollywood lifestyle, he remains loyal to his friends and family back home. He still has the most fun hanging out with his pals, Casey and Tony. Even though Ryan's been spending more and more time on the road, he still loves coming home to his family and friends.

# Get to Know Ryan's Friends

## Casey

★ Ryan's best friend

★ Stood by Ryan as both of their families went through a divorce at the same time (and Ryan stood by him!)

★ Currently attending a college near his home of San Clemente, California

★ Loves skating, surfing, wakeboarding, and motocross

★ A mellow guy and loyal pal

## Tony

★ Ryan's skating bro

★ A very skilled skateboarder, sponsored by Oakley and Etnies

★ The most dramatic and outspoken guy of the crew

★ Known for being a major flirt

★ Friends with Ryan since the sixth grade

## Taylor

✷ Casey's on again-off again girlfriend

✷ Doesn't skate, but the crew considers her "one of the guys"

✷ Loves snowboarding, surfing, and playing soccer

✷ Met Ryan in their freshman computer class

✷ Great at giving Ryan advice on his love life

## Mitch

✷ Newest addition to the gang

✷ He and Ryan used to compete for the same girl . . . Mitch won!

✷ Makes a living fixing motorcycles and selling them

✷ Has already cofounded his own skateboard company

✷ Currently attending college with Casey

# Hanging with Ryan

**W**hen he's **not** practicing his tricks, one of the places you'll often find him is the beach.

Ryan and his friends all love to catch some waves, and their hometown of San Clemente, California, is a surfer's paradise. It's said that the sun shines on this beach community, located in Orange County, halfway between San Diego and Los Angeles, 342 days a year. That gives the gang plenty of opportunities to get out in the water to surf and wakeboard.

Given his love of surfing and skateboarding, it's not surprising that Ryan also loves to ride the ski slopes. When the weather's right, the crew likes to hit the slopes and get in as much snowboarding as possible. But when Ryan's asked what sport he'd enter if he couldn't skateboard, he always says he'd like to seriously compete in motocross—he and his friends have worn out the trails near his home. In fact, Ryan has a passion for cars and bikes, in general. He loves speed and all forms of competition.

[ Believe it or not, there's more to Ryan than just skateboarding. ]

He loves speed and all forms of competition.

Obviously, the skating star loves the outdoors, but that's just one of the qualities he's looking for in his friends and love interests. He's looking for a girl who's fun and active and can keep up with his high-energy lifestyle. That's not all: It's important to Ryan that the girl he dates gets along with his close-knit group of friends, so she'd have to be easygoing and spontaneous. He's attracted to girls who aren't afraid to be goofy sometimes and who don't take themselves too seriously. If a girl's into him, he wants her to show him she cares. His busy schedule doesn't allow time for head games.

While Ryan would love to find the girl of his dreams, he's still very much focused on his career and his sport. With that in mind, he's been spending more time at the gym, often working out with his dad. He exercises about four times a week and in the last year or two has added about twenty-five pounds of muscle. The added strength has made him an even tougher competitor.

Working out, playing hard, and maintaining his relationships, Ryan makes sure to keep a healthy balance and to live life to its fullest.

# All Things Ryan

You *think* you're a Ryan Sheckler fan, but how well do you know him, really? Take a minute to try out this trivia quiz and test your Sheckler knowledge. In the process, you may just find you have something in common with him!

1. **What's Ryan's nickname?**

   a. **Shecks**

   b. **Shecky**

   c. **All of the above**

   d. **None of the above**

2. What sports team did Ryan join when he attended San Clemente High?

   a. Wrestling

   b. Soccer

   c. Baseball

   d. None of the above

3. Where's Ryan's favorite place to travel?

   a. Mexico

   b. Paris

   c. Hawaii

   d. Australia

4. What's Ryan's astrological sign?

   a. Virgo—that's why he's such a perfectionist

   b. Leo—which explains his strong self-confidence

   c. Capricorn—shows why he's so hardworking and ambitious

   d. Cancer—no wonder he's so loyal to friends and family

5. Where does Ryan most like to eat out?

   a. McDonald's

   b. Olive Garden

   c. San Clemente Diner

   d. Wahoo's

6. What was Ryan's first car?

   a. Hummer

   b. Range Rover

   c. Porsche

   d. BMW

7. Which actress would Ryan most love to date?

   a. Paris Hilton

   b. Scarlett Johansson

   c. Jessica Alba

   d. Hayden Panettiere

8. Who was Ryan's first kiss?

    a. His high-school girlfriend, Cambria

    b. A fan named Lacey

    c. Kimmy, a girl in his fifth-grade class

    d. It's a secret! He won't tell!

9. What's Ryan's favorite school subject?

    a. Science

    b. Math

    c. English

    d. Spanish

10. What does Ryan consider his bad habit?

    a. Spending too much money

    b. Impatience

    c. Biting his nails

    d. All of the above

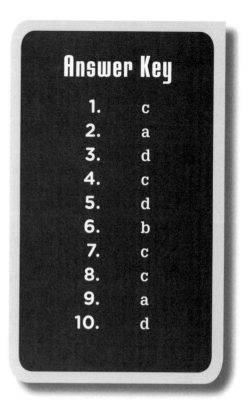

**Answer Key**

1. c
2. a
3. d
4. c
5. d
6. b
7. c
8. c
9. a
10. d

# How Did You Do?

**If you had 0 to 3 correct answers:**

Wait a minute. You know this is a *Ryan Sheckler* book, right? He's a pro skateboarder, dude, not that guy in *High School Musical*. Okay, maybe you're just a brand-new fan, but you still have lots to learn.

**If you had 4 to 7 correct answers:**

Well, that's not embarrassing, at least. You've read some articles, maybe his photo is on your screensaver. But you probably have the Jonas Brothers and Shia LaBeouf up there on your computer, too.

**If you had 8 to 10 correct answers:**

Okay . . . stalker? You are one *serious* Ryan Sheckler fan. Chances are, you know more about Ryan than any of your friends. And you know just enough about him to either be his girlfriend or have him take a restraining order out against you!

# What Ryan's Astrological Sign Says About Him . . .

**Capricorn birthdates:** December 22 to January 20

**Symbol:** The Goat

**Other famous Capricorns:** Jude Law, Jim Carrey, Orlando Bloom

**Traits:**

| | |
|---|---|
| Pessimistic | Practical |
| Reserved | Moody |
| Ambitious | Disciplined |
| Independent | Stubborn |
| Hardworking | Responsible |
| Motivated | Conservative |

**Most compatible with:** Virgo and Taurus

**Least compatible with:** Aries and Libra

# Shooting Higher

**R**yan has accomplished so much at such a young age, it's hard to imagine what he might want to do next.

Some of Ryan's future plans involve giving back.

Just this year he donated his own Range Rover to raise money for Children's Cancer Research Fund. The car went to the donor who raised the most funds for that worthy organization. In addition, he and his brothers launched the Sheckler Family Foundation.

Ryan has said, "With this foundation I intend to fund causes that are dear to my heart: pediatric cancer research, finding a cure for spinal cord injuries, and funding programs in underprivileged communities."

That said, there's still a few things he'd like to achieve in his skating career. One of those goals is being named Skater of the Year, an annual title given out by *Thrasher* magazine and chosen by its readers. Since its introduction in 1990, the award has become one of the most respected in pro skateboarding. The very first Skater of the Year was Ryan's idol, Tony Hawk.

In addition to winning more competitions, Ryan's also interested in running his own businesses. He's said that he'll probably keep skating professionally until he's about thirty. After that, he wants to control some companies that are directly and indirectly related to the sport. The skating world will always be in his blood.

When considering his future, Ryan always looks to the advice and example of his mentors. Rodney Mullen, Ronnie Creager, Jamie Thomas, and Tony Hawk are all guys who have had amazing skating careers and Ryan's always looked up to them. He hopes to one day be a hero to other young skaters like his mentors have been to him. But we know, he already is!

# Get to Know Ryan's Idols

## Rodney Mullen

★ Known as the most influential skateboarder ever

★ Nicknamed "Mutt" and "King"

★ Invented a ton of tricks that are performed regularly by competitive skaters today

★ Turned pro in 1980

★ Created the Almost skateboard company in 2002

## Ronnie Creager

★ One of the most gifted skateboarders in the world

★ Best known for his technical skating and manual and ledge tricks

★ Often plays golf with Ryan

★ Turned pro in 1992

★ Known for his mellow, laid-back attitude

# Jamie Thomas

- One of the most recognized pros on today's skating scene

- Nicknamed "The Chief"

- First started skateboarding as a way to get to school

- Turned pro when he was eighteen

- Best known for attempting the "Leap of Faith"—a dangerous two-story jump that he never quite landed

# Tony Hawk

- The most famous skateboarder of our time

- Nicknamed "Birdman"

- Known for landing the first 900—two-and-a-half rotations in the air—in a competition

- Turned pro at age fourteen

- Owns several companies and has loaned his name to things like books, video games, and even roller coasters

# RYAN:
## Up Close and Personal

- One accessory he always keeps with him: **Chap-Stick**

- The cell phone brand he uses: **Blackberry**

- One of his favorite movies: *Anchorman*

- His dream car: **Ferrari 430**

- The game he plays with his friends: **Guitar Hero**

- His favorite fast food: **In-N-Out Burger**

- A magazine he subscribes to that *isn't* about skateboarding: *Rolling Stone*

- His favorite home-cooked dinner: **Steak**

- His favorite cartoon: *South Park*

- What most fans don't know about him: **He has Attention Deficit Disorder**

"I can see people being skeptical about a skateboarder getting a reality show, but they need to open their eyes and realize that if you're given an opportunity to do something different and something sick, who am I or anybody else to tell someone to turn it down."

"I'm always training, always thinking about skateboarding."

# So Who Is Ryan Sheckler, Anyway?

*J*ust like any other public figure, Ryan has his true fans and he has his haters. There are hardcore skaters—even other pros—who think skateboarding should remain an edgy, rebellious activity. They think that with his show and celebrity, Ryan has sold out and ruined the sport.

Ryan brushes off the negativity. He's proud of what he's accomplished and what he's brought to skateboarding: "I've introduced skateboarding to kids out there that never ever wanted to skateboard. So how is that ruining skateboarding?" By popularizing the sport, Ryan is actually helping out other pro skaters. Sales for their sponsored products are on the rise, so everybody wins.

So who is Ryan, really?

He's a loving son,

devoted brother,

loyal friend,

talented athlete,

ambitious businessman, and **HOT** colebrity.

But best of all, he's just a regular guy— and that's what makes him Ryan Sheckler.

# Ryan Stats

**Birth Date:** December 30, 1989

**Height:** 5' 8"

**Weight:** 130 pounds

**Hair Color:** brown

**Eye Color:** green

**Middle Name:** Allen

**Started Skating:** 1993

**Began Competing:** 1997

**Turned Pro:** 2003

**Stance On a Skateboard:** Regular (left foot forward)

**Number of Sponsors:** 13

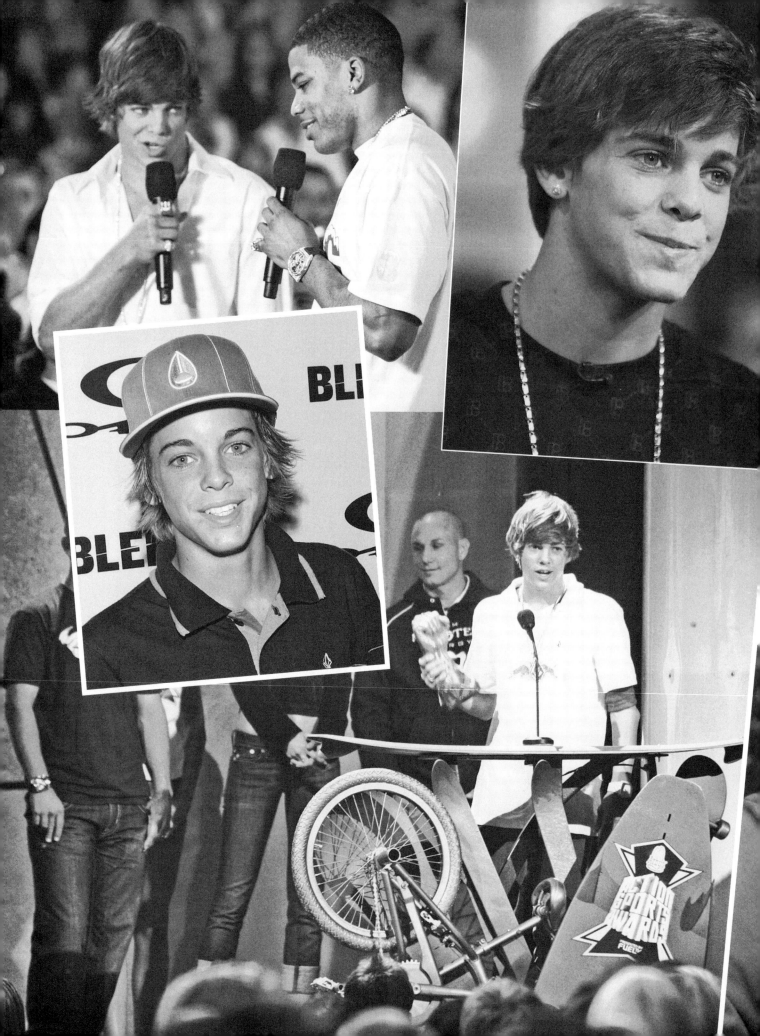

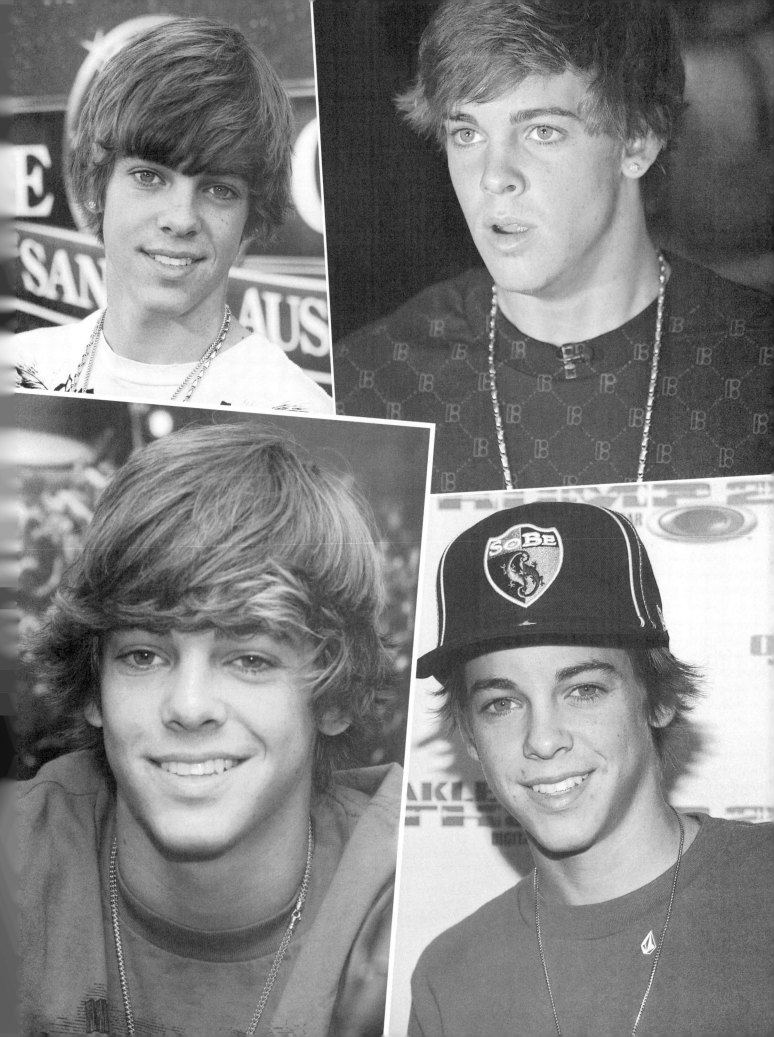